Foreword by Chico Henderson

In today's world, the dream of starting a new life in the United States is shared by millions of people around the globe. The U.S. has long been a beacon of opportunity, diversity, and growth, but navigating the immigration process to make that dream a reality can be daunting. As someone who has witnessed firsthand the complexities and challenges that come with seeking entry into this country, I understand how overwhelming it can be to take those first steps.

This book, *The Official Guide to Immigrating to the United States of America*, offers something truly valuable: clarity. It doesn't just scratch the surface of immigration or overwhelm you with jargon and legalese. Instead, it introduces all the core concepts surrounding immigration, taking you through the U.S. immigration system from A to Z. Every chapter is crafted to break down what can often feel like an impenetrable wall of bureaucracy into digestible, clear, and actionable information.

From the laws that govern immigration to the agencies responsible for processing your applications, this guide will provide you with a solid understanding of how the system works. But more than that, it will give you the tools to take the right steps toward achieving your immigration goals. After laying the foundation of knowledge, the book concludes with a step-by-step guide that explains exactly how to navigate the system and successfully get into the United States as an immigrant.

Whether you are a student seeking educational opportunities, a skilled professional looking for employment, or a family member reuniting with loved ones, this book has something for you. By the end, you will not only have a thorough understanding of U.S. immigration but also a practical guide to help you along the way.

I hope this book serves as your reliable companion on this significant journey, as you take the first steps toward building your future in the United States.

— Chico Henderson

Chapter 1: Understanding the U.S. Immigration System

Immigrating to the United States is a significant and often challenging process. It involves navigating a complex system of laws, regulations, and procedures that govern who can enter, stay, and ultimately settle in the country. Understanding this system is crucial for anyone beginning their immigration journey, as it provides the framework for the steps you'll need to take along the way. This chapter provides an overview of the U.S. immigration system, outlining key agencies, visa types, and the general immigration process.

1.1 Overview of U.S. Immigration Laws

The U.S. immigration system is primarily governed by federal laws, designed to regulate the entry, residence, and status of non-citizens. The foundational law is the **Immigration and Nationality Act (INA)**, first enacted in 1952 and amended many times since. This act sets out the rules for who may immigrate to the U.S., under what conditions, and how long they can stay.

Key Agencies Involved:

Several government agencies play critical roles in enforcing immigration laws and handling immigration processes. Each one has a unique responsibility within the broader framework of U.S. immigration:

- **U.S. Citizenship and Immigration Services (USCIS):** Part of the Department of Homeland Security (DHS), USCIS manages the process for visa applications, green card petitions, and naturalization for those seeking U.S. citizenship. USCIS is responsible for reviewing and approving or denying immigration benefits based on eligibility criteria.
- **U.S. Customs and Border Protection (CBP):** Another branch of DHS, CBP oversees the physical borders of the United States. It is responsible for inspecting and admitting individuals entering the country and ensuring compliance with customs and immigration laws. CBP officers assess travelers at U.S. ports of entry to determine whether they are admissible.
- **U.S. Immigration and Customs Enforcement (ICE):** ICE enforces immigration laws within the U.S. It focuses on identifying, apprehending, and removing individuals who violate immigration regulations. ICE also handles investigations into immigration fraud and criminal activities related to immigration law violations.
- **The Department of State (DOS):** DOS plays a critical role in the immigration process through its consulates and embassies around the world. It is responsible for processing visa applications abroad, conducting visa interviews, and making final decisions on immigrant and non-immigrant visa applications.

Together, these agencies form the backbone of the U.S. immigration system, with responsibilities ranging from border control and visa issuance to law enforcement and the processing of citizenship applications.

1.2 Types of Visas and Immigration Status

Understanding the various visa categories and immigration statuses available is key to determining the right path for your situation. Broadly, visas are divided into **non-immigrant** (temporary) and **immigrant** (permanent) categories, each with its own eligibility requirements and purposes.

Non-Immigrant Visas:

Non-immigrant visas are intended for individuals who wish to enter the U.S. on a temporary basis for a specific reason, such as tourism, education, or work. Common non-immigrant visa categories include:

- **B-1/B-2 Visas (Business/Tourism):** These visas allow individuals to visit the U.S. for short-term business purposes (B-1) or tourism and leisure (B-2).
- **F-1 Visa (Student Visa):** This visa is for individuals who wish to pursue academic studies at a U.S. institution. F-1 visa holders can study full-time and may also be eligible for limited work opportunities through Optional Practical Training (OPT) programs.
- **H-1B Visa (Specialty Occupations):** Designed for skilled workers in specialized fields, the H-1B visa allows individuals to work in the U.S. in positions requiring specialized knowledge, typically in areas like technology, engineering, or medicine.
- **J-1 Visa (Exchange Visitors):** The J-1 visa supports cultural exchange and educational programs, including internships, research, and teaching. J-1 holders are often sponsored by educational or cultural institutions.

Immigrant Visas:

Immigrant visas are for individuals seeking to live and work permanently in the United States. These visas are generally sponsored by a family member or employer, though other pathways exist. Immigrant visa categories include:

- **Family-Based Immigration:** U.S. citizens and lawful permanent residents can sponsor close relatives to immigrate. Family-based immigration includes two main categories: immediate relatives (spouses, parents, children) and family preference categories (siblings, adult children).
- **Employment-Based Immigration:** U.S. employers may sponsor foreign workers for permanent residency. This category is divided into several preference levels based on the individual's qualifications, job offer, or contributions to the U.S. economy.
- **Diversity Visa Program (Green Card Lottery):** This program provides a limited number of immigrant visas each year to individuals from countries with historically low immigration rates to the U.S. Winners of the lottery can apply for permanent residency.

Refugee and Asylee Status:

Some individuals immigrate to the U.S. seeking protection from persecution in their home countries. These categories include:

- **Refugees:** Individuals who apply from outside the U.S. for entry based on a well-founded fear of persecution due to race, religion, nationality, or political opinion.

- **Asylees:** Individuals already in the U.S. who seek protection from persecution in their home country under similar criteria as refugees.

1.3 The Immigration Process

The process of immigrating to the U.S. can vary depending on the type of visa or status you are applying for, but the general steps are similar across most categories.

1. Research and Preparation:

The first step in the immigration journey is research. It's important to determine which visa or immigration status fits your situation, considering factors like your goals, eligibility, and long-term plans.

- **Determine Eligibility:** Each visa or immigration status has specific requirements. Review the criteria carefully to ensure you meet them before proceeding.
- **Consult Resources:** Utilize trusted resources such as the USCIS website or consult with an immigration attorney to guide you through the process. Immigration laws can be complex, and professional guidance can be invaluable.

2. Application Submission:

Once you've determined which visa or status to apply for, the next step is submitting the necessary applications.

- **Complete Forms:** For immigrant visas, common forms include Form I-130 (Petition for Alien Relative) or Form I-140 (Immigrant Petition for Alien Worker). Non-immigrant visas require different forms, depending on the visa category.
- **Submit Documentation:** Each application requires supporting documents, such as proof of relationship (for family-based immigration) or job offers (for employment-based immigration). Ensure that all required documents are submitted to avoid delays.

3. Processing and Review:

After submission, your application will go through a review process. Processing times vary depending on the type of application and the current workload at USCIS or the relevant U.S. consulate.

- **Wait for Processing:** Immigration processing can take months or even years in some cases. Monitor the status of your application through official channels and be prepared for potential delays.
- **Respond to Requests:** USCIS or DOS may request additional information or documentation. Respond promptly to any requests to avoid further delays.

4. Interviews and Decision:

For many visa categories, applicants are required to attend an in-person interview.

- **Attend Interviews:** Interviews are typically conducted at a U.S. consulate or embassy for non-immigrant and immigrant visa applicants. During the interview, you will be asked about your application, background, and reasons for immigrating.
- **Receive a Decision:** Once the interview is complete, you will receive a decision on your visa application. If approved, you will be informed of the next steps for entering the U.S.

5. Final Steps:

If your application is successful, you will be issued a visa or green card, allowing you to enter the U.S.

- **Visa Issuance:** You will receive a visa if you applied for a non-immigrant or immigrant visa abroad. For green card holders, you may be granted conditional or permanent residency, depending on the circumstances of your case.
- **Prepare for Entry:** Once your visa is issued, follow any final instructions for entering the U.S. and begin preparing for your move, including setting up housing, securing employment, and understanding U.S. laws and customs.

Conclusion

Navigating the U.S. immigration system can be daunting, but understanding the basic framework can make the process more manageable. By familiarizing yourself with the key agencies, visa categories, and steps involved, you can approach your immigration journey with greater confidence. The next chapters will provide in-depth guidance on specific immigration paths and how to prepare for each stage of your application.

End of Chapter 1.

Chapter 2: Preparing for Immigration

Immigrating to the United States is a transformative journey that requires thorough preparation. The process involves multiple steps, from selecting the right visa to gathering essential documents and understanding the costs involved. Preparation is key to ensuring that your immigration journey is as smooth and stress-free as possible. This chapter will provide a detailed guide on how to approach these crucial steps and set yourself up for success as you embark on your path toward becoming a U.S. immigrant.

2.1 Researching and Choosing a Visa

The first and arguably most important step in your immigration journey is selecting the appropriate visa. The U.S. offers various visa categories tailored to different purposes—employment, education, family reunification, and permanent residency. Each category has specific eligibility criteria, benefits, and restrictions. Therefore, understanding your options and identifying the visa that best suits your situation is crucial.

1. Identifying Your Purpose

The purpose of your immigration will largely determine which visa you should apply for. Here's a breakdown of the common visa purposes:

- **Employment**: If your goal is to work in the U.S., there are several employment-based visa options. The most popular is the **H-1B** visa, which is for individuals in specialized occupations, such as engineers, scientists, and IT professionals. The **L-1 visa** is available for intra-company transferees who are moving from a branch of their current employer abroad to a U.S. office.
- **Education**: If you plan to study in the U.S., the **F-1 visa** is typically used for students attending academic institutions like universities, while the **J-1 visa** is for exchange visitors participating in internships, training programs, or cultural exchanges.
- **Family Reunification**: If you have immediate family members who are U.S. citizens or lawful permanent residents, you may be eligible for family-based visas. The **Immediate Relative (IR)** visa category applies to spouses, parents, and children of U.S. citizens, while **Family Preference (F)** visas are for more distant relatives.
- **Permanent Residency**: Those seeking permanent residency can explore options like the **EB-5 investor visa**, which is for individuals who invest a significant amount of capital in a U.S. business, or the **Diversity Visa Program (DV Lottery)**, which offers permanent residency to individuals from countries with historically low U.S. immigration rates.

2. Reviewing Visa Requirements

Each visa type has its own eligibility criteria and application process. Before committing to a visa application, it's essential to thoroughly research the requirements and ensure that you meet them. Here are a few key points to consider:

- **Eligibility Criteria**: Different visas have different criteria. For employment visas, you may need to demonstrate specialized skills or a job offer from a U.S. employer. Family-based visas require proof of a legitimate familial relationship

with a U.S. citizen or permanent resident. Understanding these requirements in advance will save you time and avoid costly mistakes.
- **Application Process**: The visa application process can vary depending on the category. Some visas, such as employment-based visas, may require sponsorship from a U.S. employer, while others, like the Diversity Visa Program, involve a lottery system with strict deadlines. Make sure you understand the steps involved, including forms to complete and fees to pay.
- **Supporting Documents**: Visa applications require specific documentation to prove your eligibility. For example, you may need to provide a job offer letter, proof of family relationship, or educational transcripts. Review the list of required documents for your chosen visa and start gathering them early.

3. Consulting Official Resources

It's always wise to consult official and trusted resources when preparing for immigration:

- **USCIS Website**: The U.S. Citizenship and Immigration Services (USCIS) website is the most reliable source of information for all U.S. visa categories. It provides detailed guidelines on eligibility, application processes, and forms.
- **Legal Advisors**: Given the complexities of U.S. immigration law, you may want to consult an immigration attorney for personalized advice. Legal counsel can help you navigate the process, especially if your situation is complicated or if you're unsure about the right visa for your circumstances.

2.2 Gathering Essential Documents

Once you've identified the appropriate visa, the next step is to gather the necessary documentation. Proper documentation is essential for a smooth immigration process. Incomplete or incorrect documents can result in delays, rejections, or even bans. This section will help you prepare your documents effectively.

1. Personal Identification Documents

Your personal identification documents are fundamental to your visa application:

- **Passport**: Ensure your passport is valid for at least six months beyond your intended stay in the U.S. It's best to renew your passport well before it expires to avoid any last-minute complications.
- **Birth Certificate**: Some visa categories, particularly family-based visas, require a certified copy of your birth certificate to establish proof of identity and familial relationships.

2. Visa-Specific Documents

Different visa categories require different documents. Here are some examples:

- **Application Forms**: Every visa application requires you to complete specific forms. For family-based visas, this could include **Form I-130 (Petition for Alien Relative)**. For employment-based visas, it might be **Form I-140 (Immigrant Petition for Alien Worker)**. Be sure to fill out these forms accurately and double-check for any mistakes.
- **Proof of Eligibility**: You'll need to provide documents that prove you meet the eligibility criteria for your chosen visa. This might include a job offer letter from a U.S. employer, educational transcripts, or proof of a family relationship.

3. Financial Documents

Demonstrating financial stability is a key requirement for many U.S. visa categories:

- **Proof of Funds**: Some visas require applicants to prove they can support themselves financially while in the U.S. Bank statements, affidavits of support from family members, or financial sponsorship documents are commonly used for this purpose.
- **Receipt of Fees**: Be prepared to show receipts proving that you've paid all applicable visa application fees. Keep copies of all payment confirmations.

4. Additional Supporting Documents

Certain visas require additional documentation:

- **Medical Examinations**: Some visa categories require you to undergo a medical examination by a U.S. government-approved physician. Make sure to keep copies of all medical reports and vaccination records.
- **Police Certificates**: In some cases, you may need to provide police clearance certificates from countries where you have lived. These documents help demonstrate that you do not have a criminal record.

5. Document Preparation Tips

To avoid any delays or issues with your visa application, follow these tips:

- **Translations**: If any of your documents are not in English, you'll need to have them translated. Ensure that the translations are certified and include a signed statement from the translator verifying the accuracy of the translation.
- **Copies**: Make multiple copies of every document you submit. This includes forms, passports, birth certificates, proof of funds, and medical reports. Keep the originals in a safe place and submit only the copies unless otherwise requested.

2.3 Understanding the Costs

Immigrating to the U.S. can be an expensive endeavor, and understanding the costs involved will help you avoid any surprises. There are a variety of fees associated with different aspects of the immigration process, from application fees to travel expenses.

1. Application Fees

Visa applications come with associated fees that vary depending on the type of visa you are applying for:

- **Visa Application Fees**: The application fee for a visa can range from a few hundred to several thousand dollars. For example, the application fee for an H-1B visa is different from that of a family-based immigrant visa. Check the current fee schedule on the USCIS website or the U.S. consulate or embassy in your country.
- **Biometrics Fee**: Some visa types require applicants to pay an additional fee for biometrics, such as fingerprints and photographs. This fee is typically required for certain immigration statuses, including green cards and work permits.

2. Additional Costs

Beyond the application fees, there are several other costs to consider:

- **Legal Fees**: If you hire an immigration attorney to assist with your application, be sure to factor in legal fees. Attorney fees can vary depending on the complexity of your case and the services provided. While legal assistance is not required, it can be beneficial for navigating complex situations.
- **Medical Exam Fees**: Some visas require medical examinations, which are conducted by approved doctors. The fees for these exams vary by country and medical facility.
- **Travel Costs**: Depending on your visa type, you may need to travel to a U.S. consulate or embassy for an interview. Be sure to budget for airfare, accommodations, and other travel-related expenses.

3. Budgeting and Planning

To ensure that you are financially prepared for your immigration journey, it's essential to create a budget:

- **Create a Budget**: Start by listing all the potential costs, including application fees, legal fees, travel expenses, and any additional charges related to your specific visa type. Add a buffer for any unexpected expenses.
- **Monitor Changes**: Immigration fees and requirements can change over time. Stay informed about any updates that might affect your costs by regularly checking the USCIS website and other official sources.

2.4 Tips for Successful Preparation

Successfully preparing for immigration involves more than just gathering documents and paying fees. Staying organized, starting early, and seeking help when needed are key strategies to ensure your application process goes smoothly.

1. Stay Organized

Staying organized is essential for managing the complexities of the immigration process:

- **Create a Checklist**: Develop a comprehensive checklist that includes all the required documents and steps for your visa application. Check off items as you complete them to stay on track.
- **Use a Filing System**: Keep all your immigration-related documents in one place, such as a binder or a digital folder. Label everything clearly to make it easy to find when needed.

2. Start Early

The immigration process can take time, and starting early will help you avoid unnecessary stress:

- **Begin Documentation Early**: Some documents, such as police certificates or medical exam results, may take weeks or even months to obtain. Start gathering these documents as soon as you decide to apply for a visa.

3. Seek Assistance

Don't hesitate to seek help if you need it:

- **Ask for Legal Advice**: If you are unsure about any aspect of the visa application process, consulting an immigration attorney can provide valuable guidance.
- **Use Online Resources**: Many online forums and communities offer advice and support to individuals going through the immigration process. These resources can provide insights and tips from others who have successfully navigated the system.

Conclusion

By researching visa options, gathering essential documents, understanding the costs involved, and staying organized, you can approach the immigration process with confidence. Careful preparation will set you on the right path to achieve your goal of immigrating to the U.S.

End of Chapter 2.

Chapter 3: The Application Process

The application process for immigrating to the United States is a pivotal step in your journey toward a new life. Although the procedures can seem overwhelming, understanding each part of the process will help you navigate it with confidence and precision. This chapter will provide you with detailed guidance on filling out applications, submitting them correctly, preparing for interviews, and knowing what to expect in the decision-making phase. With the right preparation, you can increase your chances of a smooth, successful experience.

3.1 Filling Out Applications

The first step in the immigration process is completing the necessary forms, which are determined by the visa type you're pursuing. This section outlines how to select the right forms, complete them accurately, and gather supporting documents for submission.

3.1.1 Selecting the Correct Forms

The U.S. immigration system is multifaceted, and different visa categories require different forms. Choosing the correct forms is crucial, as applying with the wrong forms can delay your case or even lead to denial.

- **Identify Required Forms**: The type of visa you're applying for will dictate which forms you need to complete. Here's a brief overview:
    - **Family-Based Visas**: If you're applying for a visa through a family member who is a U.S. citizen or permanent resident, you'll likely need to fill out **Form I-130**, which is the "Petition for Alien Relative." This form establishes the familial relationship and initiates the immigration process for your relative.
    - **Employment-Based Visas**: For those coming to the U.S. to work, the employer generally files **Form I-140**, known as the "Immigrant Petition for Alien Worker." This form demonstrates that the employer has a legitimate job offer for you and that you meet the qualifications for the position.
    - **Student Visas**: If you're planning to study in the U.S., you will need **Form DS-160**, the "Online Nonimmigrant Visa Application." This is an online form required for most nonimmigrant visas and serves as your official application to study in the United States.

- **Diversity Visa Lottery**: For those entering the Diversity Visa Lottery, the application process is somewhat different. The first step is to complete the electronic entry form on the U.S. Department of State's Diversity Visa Lottery website. Winners of the lottery are then directed to fill out additional forms.
- **Obtain Forms**: You can download most forms from the **USCIS website** or the **U.S. Department of State website**. Alternatively, U.S. embassies and consulates provide these forms, or you can request them through mail services. Ensure you are downloading the most current version of the form, as outdated forms can cause delays or rejections.

3.1.2 Completing Forms Accurately

Accuracy is key when filling out any immigration application. Simple mistakes, omissions, or discrepancies can lead to processing delays or denials, so it's essential to take your time and ensure that every detail is correct.

- **Follow Instructions**: Every immigration form comes with a set of instructions that outlines how to complete it. Read the instructions thoroughly before starting. Some forms may seem straightforward, but small mistakes can have large consequences. For instance, not signing a form or using incorrect dates can cause significant delays in your case.
- **Provide Complete Information**: Each section of the form must be filled out completely. For family-based visas, this includes detailed personal information about you and your relative (petitioner). For employment-based visas, you will need to provide information about the employer, job offer, and your qualifications. Missing sections or incomplete answers can lead to requests for additional information, which could prolong the process.
- **Avoid Mistakes**: Double-check all entries before submitting the form. Look out for common mistakes, such as incorrect names, dates, or immigration history. Remember that errors or contradictions in your forms could lead to requests for further documentation or even result in denial. For example, ensure the personal details on all documents match exactly (including passport, birth certificate, and any other identification).

3.1.3 Supporting Documentation

Along with the forms, supporting documentation is often required to substantiate your claims. Gathering and organizing these documents beforehand will help streamline the process.

- **Compile Required Documents**: Different visas require different supporting documents. Here are examples of what may be needed for various visa types:
  - **Proof of Relationship**: For family-based visas, you'll need documents proving your relationship with the petitioner, such as birth certificates, marriage certificates, or adoption papers.

- o **Employment Evidence**: For employment-based visas, you'll need letters from your employer, tax forms, or other proof that you have a legitimate job offer. These documents should establish both the existence of the job and your qualifications.
- o **Financial Documents**: Some visas require proof of financial stability. This could be bank statements, tax returns, or affidavits of support from your sponsor.
- **Organize Documents**: Follow the instructions on the forms regarding the order and format of documents. For example, some applications may require documents to be stapled or grouped in a specific order. Having your documents in the right order helps the immigration officer process your application more quickly and reduces the likelihood of your file being returned for corrections.

3.2 Submitting Your Application

Once you've filled out your application and gathered the necessary documents, it's time to submit your application. Where and how you submit it depends on the type of visa and your location.

3.2.1 Where to Submit

- **USCIS Applications**: If you're applying from within the U.S., your application will be submitted to a **USCIS Service Center**. These centers process various types of immigration applications. The form instructions will tell you which center to send your application to, based on the type of visa you're applying for.
- **Consular Applications**: If you're applying from outside the U.S., you'll need to submit your application to the **U.S. embassy or consulate** in your country. Each consulate has its own process for submitting visa applications, so be sure to check the specific instructions for your location.

3.2.2 Submission Methods

- **Online Submission**: Many applications can be submitted online via the **USCIS** or **Department of State** websites. Online submission typically allows for faster processing, as documents can be uploaded and fees paid digitally. Follow all online instructions carefully to ensure your submission is successful.
- **Mailing Paper Applications**: If you're submitting a paper application, ensure you use the correct mailing address listed in the form's instructions. It's recommended to use a **secure mailing method** that allows for tracking, such as certified mail or a courier service, so you have proof of submission and can track its progress.

3.2.3 Tracking and Confirmation

- **Receipt Notices**: Once your application is received, you will be sent a **receipt notice** containing your **case number**. This number is essential for tracking your application status and for any future correspondence with USCIS or the consulate. Keep this notice in a safe place for future reference.
- **Tracking Status**: Both USCIS and U.S. consulates provide online portals where you can track the status of your application. With your case number, you can log in and see updates on your application's progress.

3.3 Interview Preparation

For many visa types, an interview is a required part of the process. This is your opportunity to clarify any aspects of your application and demonstrate your eligibility for the visa.

3.3.1 Scheduling the Interview

- **Appointment Notice**: If an interview is required, you will receive an appointment notice detailing the date, time, and location. Follow all instructions provided in this notice carefully, as missing or being late to your interview can seriously delay or jeopardize your application.
- **Rescheduling**: If you cannot attend the scheduled interview, contact the appropriate agency or consulate as soon as possible to request a reschedule. Rescheduling options may be limited, and failing to attend could result in your application being denied.

3.3.2 Preparing for the Interview

Preparation is key to a successful interview. Review your application thoroughly and make sure you are ready to answer any questions the interviewer may have.

- **Review Your Application**: The interviewer may ask you specific questions based on the information you provided in your application. Review your forms and supporting documents so you can provide accurate answers.
- **Practice Common Questions**: Different visa types have different interview questions. For example:
    - **Family-Based Visas**: You may be asked about your relationship with the petitioner, including how and when you met, your living situation, and any other relevant personal information.
    - **Employment-Based Visas**: Expect questions about the job you've been offered, your qualifications, and the company offering you the position.
    - **Student Visas**: You may be asked about your study plans, the institution you're attending, and how you plan to fund your education.
- **Gather Additional Documents**: Bring original copies of all supporting documents, as well as any updates or additional information requested in your

appointment notice. This might include financial statements, medical records, or proof of relationship or employment.

3.3.3 During the Interview

The interview itself is your chance to make a good impression and demonstrate that you meet all the requirements for the visa.

- **Be Honest and Clear**: Answer all questions truthfully and to the best of your ability. If you do not know the answer to a question, it's better to say so than to guess or provide inaccurate information.
- **Stay Calm and Professional**: Approach the interview with confidence, but also with professionalism. Interviews can be stressful, but staying calm and composed will help you present yourself well.

3.4 Post-Interview and Decision

After your interview, the next phase is waiting for a decision on your visa application. Here's what to expect during this phase.

3.4.1 Administrative Processing

In some cases, your application may require additional administrative processing before a final decision is made. This can happen for a variety of reasons, such as the need for additional background checks or verification of documents.

- **Timeframes**: Administrative processing can delay your case by several weeks or even months, depending on the complexity of the case. The consulate or USCIS will notify you if further processing is required.
- **Requests for Additional Evidence**: If USCIS or the consulate requires more information, you may receive a **Request for Evidence (RFE)**. Respond to these requests promptly and provide all requested documentation to avoid further delays.

3.4.2 Receiving a Decision

Once your application has been processed, you will receive a decision. If your visa is approved, you will be provided with instructions on how to proceed with obtaining your visa and entering the U.S.

- **Visa Approval**: If your visa is approved, you will either receive your visa through mail or be instructed to pick it up from the consulate or embassy. The visa will be placed in your passport, and you will be given a date by which you must enter the U.S.

- **Visa Denial**: If your visa is denied, you will be informed of the reasons for the denial. Common reasons include insufficient documentation, failure to meet eligibility requirements, or providing inaccurate information during the application process. In some cases, you may be able to appeal or reapply after addressing the reasons for the denial.

Conclusion

Navigating the application process can be complex, but with careful attention to detail and preparation, you can increase your chances of success. The next chapter will cover what to do after receiving your visa, including preparing for your move to the U.S. and what to expect upon arrival.

End of Chapter 3.

Chapter 4: Arriving and Settling in the U.S.

Arriving in the United States marks the beginning of a new chapter in your life—a time filled with excitement, challenges, and adjustments. This chapter provides a comprehensive guide to navigating the essential aspects of arriving in the U.S. and successfully settling into your new environment. By the end of this chapter, you'll be well-equipped with the knowledge and tools necessary to establish yourself in your new home, adapt to the culture, and build a solid foundation for your future.

4.1 Upon Arrival

The moment you land in the United States, you'll go through several critical procedures that ensure you are legally admitted to the country and granted the correct immigration status. It's crucial to be well-prepared for this process to avoid unnecessary complications.

4.1.1 Entry Procedures

Customs and Immigration Inspection:

After stepping off the plane, the first stop is U.S. Customs and Border Protection (CBP). CBP officers are responsible for reviewing your entry documents and determining your eligibility to enter the U.S. Have your **passport**, **visa**, and any additional documentation—such as an invitation letter or proof of financial support—ready to present.

CBP officers will ask you a series of questions related to your travel purpose and duration of stay. Be truthful and clear in your answers. Typical questions include:

- Why are you visiting the United States?
- How long do you plan to stay?
- Where will you be staying during your visit?

While these questions may seem routine, the officer is evaluating whether you meet the entry requirements of your visa type. Inconsistencies or misleading statements can lead to complications or denial of entry.

Biometrics and Interviews:

Depending on your visa type, you may be required to undergo **biometric screening**, which involves taking your fingerprints and a photograph. This process is standard for many international travelers and helps verify your identity. In some cases, CBP officers may ask you to step into a secondary inspection room for further questioning, especially if additional clarification or document verification is needed.

This process might seem intimidating, but staying calm and providing honest answers will help you navigate it smoothly. If everything checks out, you'll be allowed to continue into the U.S.

4.1.2 Receiving Your Immigration Status

Visa Stamping:

Once you pass through immigration inspection, your visa will be stamped, officially granting you entry into the U.S. If you're entering on an immigrant visa, you'll receive a **sealed immigration packet**, which you must present to U.S. Citizenship and Immigration Services (USCIS) as part of your admission process.

Green Card Issuance:

For those entering the U.S. as permanent residents, your **green card** will not be issued immediately at the port of entry. Instead, it will be mailed to your U.S. address. Make sure USCIS has your correct address to avoid any delays in receiving your green card, as this document is crucial for proving your legal permanent resident status.

4.2 Adjusting to Life in the U.S.

Once you've successfully entered the United States, the next step is acclimating to your new environment. The U.S. is diverse, and each region has its unique culture and atmosphere, so it's important to remain adaptable and patient throughout this process.

4.2.1 Finding Housing

Temporary Accommodation:

Your first priority is likely securing temporary accommodation. You may need to stay in a hotel, short-term rental, or even with family or friends while you search for a permanent home. Ensure that your temporary housing is conveniently located near essential amenities such as public transportation, grocery stores, and your workplace or school. Online platforms like Airbnb or temporary apartment rentals can help you find suitable short-term housing options.

Long-Term Housing:

Once you've settled in, start looking for more permanent housing. This could mean renting an apartment or purchasing a home, depending on your financial situation and long-term plans. When searching for housing, consider factors such as:

- **Location:** Proximity to work, schools, public transportation, and other essential services.
- **Cost:** Be aware of rental rates in different neighborhoods. Some areas may have higher costs of living.
- **Lease Terms:** Understand the terms of any rental agreement before signing. Be clear about rental duration, rent increases, and maintenance responsibilities.

Utilize real estate websites like Zillow, Trulia, and Craigslist, and consider seeking assistance from a local real estate agent familiar with the housing market in your area.

4.2.2 Opening a Bank Account

Having a local bank account is vital for managing your finances, especially for receiving payments, paying bills, and managing day-to-day expenses.

Choosing a Bank:

Research various **banks** and **credit unions** to find one that suits your needs. Factors to consider include:

- **Fees:** Check for monthly maintenance fees, ATM fees, and minimum balance requirements.
- **Accessibility:** Look for a bank with branches and ATMs near your home or workplace.
- **Services:** Some banks offer services like overdraft protection, mobile banking, and international wire transfers, which may be essential for you.

Required Documents:

To open a U.S. bank account, you'll typically need to provide the following documents:

- Passport
- Visa or immigration documents
- Proof of U.S. address (utility bill, lease, etc.)
- Individual Taxpayer Identification Number (ITIN) or Social Security Number (SSN), if applicable.

Having a bank account will make financial transactions easier, whether it's receiving a paycheck or paying for utilities.

4.2.3 Obtaining a Social Security Number (SSN)

An SSN is essential for anyone who plans to work in the U.S. or engage in other financial activities like opening bank accounts, obtaining credit cards, or filing taxes.

Application Process:

To apply for an SSN, visit your local **Social Security Administration (SSA)** office. You'll need to bring documents proving your identity and immigration status, such as:

- Passport
- Visa or green card
- Proof of age (birth certificate)
-

Using Your SSN:

Your SSN is important for employment, paying taxes, and accessing government services. Make sure to keep your SSN card safe, as identity theft is a serious concern in the U.S.

4.3 Understanding Legal Obligations

Becoming a resident of the United States comes with specific legal responsibilities. Failing to adhere to these obligations can result in penalties or even jeopardize your immigration status.

4.3.1 Immigration Status Responsibilities

Compliance with Visa Conditions:

Each visa type has its own set of conditions, such as work restrictions or duration of stay. It's crucial to understand and follow the rules associated with your visa. For instance, certain visas prohibit full-time work without specific authorization, while others may require you to report changes in employment or residence to USCIS.

If you violate the terms of your visa, you may face serious consequences, including deportation. To avoid this, always stay informed about the conditions of your visa and consult with an immigration attorney if you have any doubts.

Status Adjustments:

Over time, you may need to adjust your immigration status or extend your stay. Whether you're applying for a green card, changing visa categories, or extending your stay, it's essential to submit your application well in advance of any deadlines. Missing a deadline or failing to apply for an extension can result in your visa being canceled or your status lapsing.

4.3.2 Legal and Tax Obligations

Tax Filing:

All U.S. residents, including immigrants, are required to file annual **tax returns**. Understanding the U.S. tax system is crucial, as your income, assets, and financial transactions are subject to taxation. The Internal Revenue Service (IRS) may require you to report foreign assets or income earned abroad.

If you're unfamiliar with U.S. tax laws, consider seeking assistance from a **tax professional** who can guide you through the process and help you file your taxes correctly.

Health Insurance:

Health insurance is a significant part of life in the U.S. Depending on your visa or residency status, you may be required to have health insurance coverage. The **Affordable Care Act (ACA)** mandates that individuals maintain health insurance or pay a penalty, although this varies by state.

Options for obtaining health insurance include:

- Employer-provided health plans
- Government programs like **Medicare** and **Medicaid**
- Private insurance plans purchased through the **Health Insurance Marketplace**

Understanding your healthcare options is critical, as medical care in the U.S. can be expensive without insurance.

4.3.3 Legal Rights and Protections

Know Your Rights:

As a resident or immigrant in the U.S., you have certain legal rights, including:

- **Employment rights:** Protection against workplace discrimination and exploitation.

- **Housing rights:** Safeguards against discrimination based on race, religion, or nationality.
- **Due process:** The right to a fair legal process if you are accused of a crime or face deportation.

Seeking Legal Help:

If you encounter legal challenges or require immigration advice, seek assistance from a qualified **immigration attorney** or a **legal aid organization**. Many non-profit organizations offer legal services for immigrants at reduced rates or free of charge.

4.4 Finding Employment and Educational Opportunities

Securing employment or pursuing education are two major aspects of settling into life in the U.S. Understanding the job market and educational system will help you build a successful future.

4.4.1 Employment

Job Search:

Your first step in finding employment is updating your **resume** to U.S. standards. This typically means highlighting your skills and achievements in a clear, concise format. Tailor your resume to each job you apply for, focusing on the qualifications and experience relevant to the position.

Job Boards:

Popular job search websites include **Indeed**, **LinkedIn**, and **Glassdoor**, where you can filter jobs by location, industry, and salary. Additionally, local **career centers** and **employment agencies** can assist you in finding work.

Work Authorization:

Before starting work, ensure that you have the necessary work authorization. Some visa types (such as student visas) require special permissions like **Optional Practical Training (OPT)** before you can begin working.

4.4.2 Education

Enrolling in Educational Programs:

If you're planning to pursue education in the U.S., research the requirements for enrollment at various institutions. Whether you're attending college or vocational training, most schools require:

- Proof of your immigration status (visa, green card, etc.)
- Academic transcripts from your home country
- Standardized test scores (e.g., TOEFL, SAT, GRE)

Scholarships and Financial Aid:

Many U.S. universities offer scholarships and financial aid to international students. Research available opportunities and reach out to **admissions offices** for guidance on how to apply.

4.5 Building a Support Network

Creating a strong support network is essential for adjusting to life in a new country. This section explores how to build personal and professional relationships that will help you navigate your new environment.

4.5.1 Community Organizations

Numerous immigrant support groups and organizations exist to help newcomers settle into life in the U.S. These organizations often provide services such as:

- English language classes
- Legal assistance
- Job placement services
- Cultural orientation programs

Getting involved with local community groups can also help you meet people who share similar backgrounds and experiences.

4.5.2 Social Integration

Meeting New People:

Making new friends and connections is key to feeling at home in your new country. Consider attending local events, joining social groups, or volunteering in your community. These activities provide opportunities to meet new people, practice English, and learn more about American culture.

Cultural Adaptation:

It's normal to experience some level of **culture shock** when moving to a new country. Be patient with yourself and allow time to adjust to different customs, values, and norms. Seeking support from other immigrants, engaging with local culture, and maintaining an open mind will help you through this transition

Conclusion

Arriving in the U.S. and settling in is a significant life change that requires careful planning and adaptability. By following the steps outlined in this chapter—preparing for entry, adjusting to life in a new country, fulfilling legal responsibilities, and building a support network—you'll be well on your way to establishing a fulfilling and successful life in the United States.

In the next chapter, we'll delve into the specifics of **navigating the U.S. healthcare system** and understanding how to access essential services, from medical care to social services, in your new home.

End of Chapter 4.

Chapter 5: Maintaining Your Immigration Status and Long-Term Planning

Maintaining your immigration status and planning for your long-term future in the United States are essential to ensuring a smooth and lawful stay. Whether you're on a temporary visa, seeking permanent residency, or aiming to become a U.S. citizen, there are key responsibilities and strategic steps you need to follow. In this chapter, we will discuss the importance of adhering to visa conditions, pathways to permanent residency and citizenship, and strategies for long-term success in the U.S.

5.1 Maintaining Your Immigration Status

1. Adhering to Visa Conditions

The first and most important step in maintaining your legal status is to understand the conditions of your visa and comply with them. U.S. immigration law is stringent, and even minor violations can lead to penalties or deportation. Different visa types have distinct requirements, and it is essential to be aware of them to avoid jeopardizing your status.

- **Understand Visa Requirements**: Each visa type has specific conditions. For instance, an H-1B work visa has different restrictions compared to a student visa (F-1), tourist visa (B-2), or investor visa (E-2). For instance, student visa holders (F-1) must maintain full-time enrollment in an accredited educational institution, while tourist visa holders cannot seek employment in the U.S. Violating these

requirements could lead to the cancellation of your visa or future ineligibility for other immigration benefits.
- **Work and Study Restrictions**: Most non-immigrant visas impose work and study restrictions. For instance, F-1 visa holders can typically work on-campus for up to 20 hours per week during the academic year, but not off-campus without proper authorization like Optional Practical Training (OPT). Similarly, H-1B visa holders must work for the employer listed on their visa application. Failing to adhere to these restrictions could result in severe consequences, including deportation.

2. Reporting Changes

Immigration authorities in the U.S. require visa holders to notify them of specific changes during their stay. These requirements are not only legal obligations but also critical to ensuring that your visa status remains in good standing.

- **Update Address**: It is your responsibility to notify U.S. Citizenship and Immigration Services (USCIS) of any change in your address within a specific timeframe—usually within 10 days. Failing to do so can result in penalties, and in some cases, jeopardize your immigration status. This rule applies to all visa holders and even lawful permanent residents.
- **Notify Changes in Employment or School**: Many visa categories, such as H-1B (work visa) or F-1 (student visa), require you to report significant changes in employment or educational status. For example, if you change employers while on an H-1B visa or transfer schools while on an F-1 visa, you must update your records with USCIS or risk losing your status.

3. Visa and Status Renewals

U.S. visas and immigration statuses are not indefinite. It's vital to keep track of your visa's expiration date and start the renewal process early to avoid lapses in your status.

- **Renewal Process**: Start preparing for your visa renewal several months before your current visa or status expires. The renewal process may include gathering documents such as proof of employment, updated financial statements, and transcripts. In some cases, you may need to attend another interview at a U.S. consulate or embassy if you are abroad. Make sure to follow the renewal procedure carefully to avoid disruptions in your legal stay.
- **Documentation**: The required documentation for visa renewal typically depends on the type of visa you hold. For example, if you are renewing a work visa, you'll need updated employment verification from your employer. For a student visa, you'll need to show continued enrollment in a qualified program. If you're renewing your visa from outside the U.S., you may also need to update your biometric information and attend a new interview at the U.S. embassy or consulate.

5.2 Pathways to Permanent Residency

For many immigrants, obtaining permanent residency (commonly referred to as a green card) is the ultimate goal. It provides a stable status and opens pathways to U.S. citizenship. There are various ways to transition to permanent residency, depending on your current visa type, work situation, family relationships, or humanitarian grounds.

1. Transitioning to Permanent Residency

- **Eligibility for a Green Card**: Several routes allow you to apply for a green card. The most common include family-based sponsorship, employment-based adjustments, and humanitarian programs like asylum or refugee status. If you are on a temporary work visa (like H-1B), your employer can sponsor you for a green card if you meet the eligibility criteria. Spouses, children, and parents of U.S. citizens are also eligible for family-sponsored green cards. Those with refugee or asylum status can often apply after one year of being granted protection in the U.S.
- **Application Process**: If eligible, you'll need to submit Form I-485 (Application to Register Permanent Residence or Adjust Status). This application involves various documents such as proof of your legal entry into the U.S., financial statements, employment letters, and proof of any family relationships, depending on your pathway to residency. You may also be required to attend a biometric appointment and an interview with USCIS.

2. Adjustment of Status

Adjusting your status to permanent residency requires careful planning, documentation, and attention to detail. Here are the key steps:

- **Required Documentation**: Collect and submit all necessary documents supporting your adjustment of status application. This could include your immigration history, proof of employment or education, tax filings, financial documents, and evidence that you have maintained lawful status throughout your stay in the U.S.
- **Medical Examination**: U.S. law requires green card applicants to undergo a medical examination by a USCIS-designated civil surgeon. The purpose is to ensure that applicants are not carrying any communicable diseases and that they meet the vaccination requirements. The results of the medical exam must be submitted along with your adjustment application.

3. Addressing Issues

Immigration laws can be complicated, and you may encounter unexpected challenges during your adjustment process. Seeking the help of an experienced immigration attorney can be crucial.

- **Legal Advice**: If you face complications—such as past violations of visa conditions, criminal history, or extended periods of unlawful presence—it's highly recommended to consult with an immigration lawyer. They can guide you through complex situations and help you address any legal obstacles that may arise during the process.

5.3 Pathways to U.S. Citizenship

Becoming a U.S. citizen is often the ultimate goal for immigrants who have established their lives in the United States. Citizenship provides full rights and protections, including the ability to vote, run for public office, and access to government benefits. The naturalization process requires meeting specific requirements, such as residency duration, moral character, and passing a citizenship test.

1. Eligibility for Naturalization

- **Residency Requirements**: To apply for U.S. citizenship, you must first be a permanent resident (green card holder) for a specific period—usually five years, or three years if you're married to a U.S. citizen. During this period, you must also have spent the majority of your time physically present in the U.S.
- **Good Moral Character**: U.S. Citizenship and Immigration Services (USCIS) evaluates naturalization applicants based on "good moral character." This means adhering to U.S. laws, paying taxes, and demonstrating responsible behavior. Criminal offenses or violations of U.S. law can disqualify you from becoming a citizen.

2. Naturalization Process

- **Application**: The naturalization process starts by submitting Form N-400 (Application for Naturalization), along with required documents such as your green card, tax records, and fees. You may also need to provide biometric information and attend an interview.
- **Citizenship Test and Interview**: As part of the process, you'll be required to take a citizenship test. This exam covers U.S. history, government, and basic English language skills. You'll also have an interview with a USCIS officer, where they will review your application and ask you questions about your background and eligibility.

3. Oath of Allegiance

- **Oath Ceremony**: If approved for citizenship, the final step is to attend a naturalization ceremony, where you will take the Oath of Allegiance. This is a public declaration of loyalty to the United States and is a significant moment marking the conclusion of your journey to becoming a U.S. citizen.

5.4 Long-Term Planning and Integration

Long-term success in the U.S. goes beyond maintaining legal status. Planning for your financial, professional, and social future is essential for a fulfilling life. Here are some key considerations for long-term planning and integration into American society.

1. Financial Planning

- **Budgeting and Saving**: Effective financial management is crucial to long-term stability. Start by creating a budget that helps you track income, expenses, and savings goals. Consider long-term financial objectives such as buying a home, starting a business, or saving for retirement.
- **Tax Planning**: Understanding U.S. tax laws is essential, as the U.S. has a complex tax system. Make sure to file your annual tax returns correctly and on time. If you're unfamiliar with the system, it may be worth consulting with a tax professional who can guide you through your obligations and help you plan for future tax payments.

2. Career Development

- **Professional Growth**: Continuing education, certifications, and industry networking are essential for career growth in the U.S. Staying up-to-date with industry trends, learning new skills, and taking advantage of professional opportunities can enhance your job prospects.
- **Job Stability**: Maintaining job stability is vital, especially if your visa status is tied to employment. Keep good relationships with your employer, stay informed about changes to immigration law, and be proactive about renewing your work authorization if necessary.

3. Community Engagement

- **Social Integration**: Becoming part of your community is vital to feeling settled and connected. Engage with local activities, attend cultural or neighborhood events, and volunteer in your community. This helps build a support network, especially if you are far from family or your home country.
- **Stay Informed**: Keep yourself updated on changes to U.S. immigration policies, laws, and regulations. Subscribe to newsletters from immigration law firms or government agencies and consider joining immigrant advocacy groups. Staying

informed will help you protect your rights and maintain a smooth journey toward your long-term goals in the U.S.
-

Conclusion

Successfully maintaining your immigration status requires a combination of strict adherence to visa conditions, careful long-term planning, and the pursuit of permanent residency or citizenship. By understanding and following U.S. immigration laws, addressing potential issues early, and strategically planning for your future, you can build a stable and fulfilling life in the United States.

End of Chapter 5.

Chapter 6: Resources and Support Systems for Immigrants

Navigating life in a new country can be overwhelming, especially when adjusting to unfamiliar systems, languages, and cultural expectations. However, immigrants arriving in the United States have access to a wide range of resources and support systems designed to help them settle, thrive, and integrate into their new environment. In this chapter, we will explore various types of assistance available to immigrants, including community organizations, legal aid, government services, and financial support, all of which aim to ease your transition and enhance your success in the U.S.

6.1 Community Organizations

1. Local Immigrant Support Groups

One of the most critical resources available to immigrants is local community organizations that cater to specific immigrant populations. These organizations often provide a comprehensive suite of services tailored to immigrants' unique needs, such as legal assistance, social services, housing referrals, and cultural integration programs.

- **Overview**: Community-based immigrant support groups play an essential role in helping new arrivals navigate the complexities of life in the U.S. These organizations are well-versed in the challenges immigrants face, including

language barriers, understanding legal processes, and adjusting to a new culture. Most community organizations provide tailored support, including free or low-cost legal services, access to social services, educational programs, and assistance with employment.
- **Examples**: The **International Rescue Committee (IRC)**, known for its work with refugees, helps newcomers rebuild their lives by providing housing support, employment services, and health care access. Another vital organization is the **Mexican American Legal Defense and Educational Fund (MALDEF)**, which focuses on protecting the rights of Latino immigrants and advocating for policy changes that benefit the immigrant community. Many cities also have smaller, local organizations that cater to immigrants from specific countries or regions, offering localized assistance and cultural resources.

2. Cultural and Ethnic Associations

Cultural continuity is important for immigrants who want to maintain their heritage while adapting to a new life in the United States. Ethnic and cultural associations provide an anchor for immigrants to connect with others from similar backgrounds and foster a sense of belonging.

- **Purpose**: Cultural and ethnic associations help immigrants maintain ties to their heritage while providing support with practical matters like language translation, social services, and networking opportunities. These organizations frequently host cultural events, such as festivals and celebrations, which serve as a space for newcomers to meet others in their community and feel more at home.
- **Finding Associations**: Finding these organizations can be as simple as conducting an online search for cultural centers or ethnic organizations representing your home country or community. For instance, **The Korean American Coalition** or **The Indian American Cultural Association** provide language classes, citizenship education, and professional networking opportunities for their respective communities. Many U.S. cities, such as Los Angeles, New York, and Houston, are home to dozens of cultural organizations that cater to immigrants from specific countries or ethnic backgrounds.

3. Volunteering and Community Involvement

Volunteering offers an excellent way to become engaged in your new community while building relationships and gaining a better understanding of local customs and practices.

- **Opportunities**: There are numerous opportunities for immigrants to get involved in their local communities. From volunteering at community centers to participating in local non-profits that focus on immigration, many organizations rely on volunteers to assist with their missions. For example, organizations like **Habitat for Humanity, Meals on Wheels**, and local food banks often welcome volunteers from diverse backgrounds and provide meaningful ways for newcomers to engage with their communities.

- **Benefits**: Volunteering provides several benefits for immigrants. It offers an opportunity to practice English and gain a deeper understanding of local customs and social norms. Moreover, volunteering helps expand social networks, enabling immigrants to build connections that may lead to future employment opportunities or simply provide valuable support.

6.2 Legal Aid and Immigration Services

Navigating the U.S. immigration system can be complicated, particularly for those unfamiliar with its legal intricacies. Access to legal assistance is vital for ensuring that immigrants understand their rights and can successfully manage their immigration status.

1. Legal Assistance

- **Immigration Lawyers**: The U.S. immigration system is a complex legal landscape, often requiring expert guidance. Immigration attorneys are crucial allies in helping immigrants understand their rights, apply for visas, renew status, and avoid deportation. Lawyers can assist with various immigration issues, including asylum applications, family-based petitions, work visa extensions, and green card applications.
- **Legal Aid Organizations**: Many non-profit organizations offer free or low-cost legal services for immigrants. **The Legal Aid Society** is one such organization that provides legal representation for immigrants facing deportation or seeking asylum. Other notable organizations include **Catholic Charities**, which offers a wide range of legal services, and the **American Immigration Lawyers Association (AILA)**, which connects immigrants with reputable attorneys.

2. Navigating Legal Services

- **Choosing an Attorney**: When seeking legal assistance, it is important to choose an immigration attorney with specific expertise in the area you need. Immigrants should verify that their attorney is licensed, experienced, and has a solid reputation. Online reviews and referrals from trusted community organizations can help ensure that you choose the right lawyer.
- **Understanding Fees**: Legal representation can be expensive, so it is essential to understand the fee structure before proceeding with any legal service. Some legal aid organizations offer sliding scale fees, where the cost of services is based on your income. Others may provide free consultations or pro bono services for those who qualify.

3. Government Resources

- **USCIS and State Agencies**: The **U.S. Citizenship and Immigration Services (USCIS)** is the government agency responsible for overseeing lawful immigration to the U.S. USCIS provides a wealth of resources, including online tools, downloadable forms, and instructional guides on topics such as applying for

citizenship, renewing visas, and understanding your rights as an immigrant. Most states also have local immigration offices that offer in-person assistance.
- **Help Centers**: USCIS operates field offices and information centers throughout the country where immigrants can schedule appointments to ask questions, check on the status of their applications, or receive guidance on navigating the system.

6.3 Government and Public Services

In addition to immigration-specific services, immigrants can also access a wide range of public and social services provided by the federal, state, and local governments.

1. Accessing Public Services
- **Healthcare**: Immigrants may be eligible for various public health services, depending on their status. Many local public health clinics and community health centers offer low-cost or free medical services, regardless of immigration status. Emergency medical services are available to everyone in the U.S., and laws protect individuals from being denied emergency care based on their ability to pay.
- **Education**: Public education in the U.S. is available to all children, including immigrant children. Adult immigrants can also access a range of educational opportunities, such as **English as a Second Language (ESL)** classes, **GED programs**, and vocational training courses, many of which are offered for free or at low cost through local community colleges and adult education centers.

2. Social Services
- **Financial Assistance**: Immigrants may qualify for financial assistance programs such as **Temporary Assistance for Needy Families (TANF)**, **Supplemental Nutrition Assistance Program (SNAP)**, and other welfare services. Eligibility often depends on immigration status, length of residence, and income levels.
- **Housing Assistance**: Many immigrants face challenges finding affordable housing, especially in major cities where rental costs are high. Immigrants can access public housing programs or receive rental assistance through local housing authorities, which aim to provide affordable housing to low-income individuals and families.

3. Emergency Services
- **Understanding Your Rights**: Immigrants are entitled to access emergency services, including police, fire, and medical services. It is important to understand your rights and how to interact with emergency personnel, especially if there are

language barriers. Immigrants are protected by various laws, and emergency responders cannot deny services based on immigration status.
- **Emergency Contacts**: Keep a list of important emergency contacts, including local emergency services and immigrant support organizations that can provide assistance if needed.

6.4 Language and Integration Programs

Language is often one of the biggest challenges for immigrants in the U.S. Fortunately, there are numerous programs designed to help immigrants improve their English skills and integrate into American society.

1. Language Classes
- **ESL Programs**: **English as a Second Language (ESL)** programs are widely available across the U.S. through public schools, community colleges, and non-profit organizations. These programs provide structured language instruction to help immigrants improve their English proficiency, which is critical for employment, education, and social integration.
- **Language Exchange Programs**: Some communities offer language exchange programs, where immigrants can practice their English skills while helping others learn their native language. These programs provide a more informal and interactive way to learn the language while building relationships with locals.

2. Cultural Orientation
- **Orientation Sessions**: Many organizations offer cultural orientation programs for new immigrants. These sessions often cover important topics such as U.S. laws, social norms, and everyday living. The **International Organization for Migration (IOM)**, for example, provides cultural orientation classes to help refugees understand life in the U.S.
- **Online Resources**: Numerous online resources are available to help immigrants acclimate to U.S. culture. Websites and platforms such as **USAHello** provide information on American etiquette, legal rights, and practical tips for daily life.

3. Networking and Social Integration
- **Local Events**: Attending local events, festivals, and social gatherings is a great way for immigrants to integrate into their new community. Many cities host multicultural events that celebrate diversity and provide opportunities for newcomers to connect with others.
- **Online Communities**: The internet offers a wealth of online communities where immigrants can seek advice, share experiences, and connect with others in similar situations. Websites and social media groups focused on immigrant issues provide support, information, and resources.

6.5 Financial Support

Financial stability is a critical factor in ensuring that immigrants can successfully integrate into their new environment. From opening bank accounts to understanding credit, financial literacy is essential for all newcomers.

1. Banking and Credit
- **Opening a Bank Account**: Having a bank account is crucial for managing your finances, especially if you plan to work in the U.S. Many banks offer accounts specifically for immigrants, even those without Social Security numbers, as long as they have valid identification.
- **Building Credit**: Establishing a credit history is important for securing loans, renting an apartment, and even getting certain jobs. Immigrants can begin building credit by applying for a secured credit card or becoming an authorized user on a relative's or friend's credit card.

2. Financial Literacy Programs
- **Workshops and Classes**: Many community organizations and non-profits offer financial literacy programs for immigrants. These programs cover essential topics such as budgeting, saving, credit building, and investing. Learning about U.S. financial systems is critical for long-term success and stability.
- **Resources**: Organizations such as **The Financial Clinic** and **Operation HOPE** provide free financial coaching and workshops tailored to immigrants, offering guidance on managing money, setting financial goals, and improving credit.

3. Government Assistance
- **Small Business Grants**: For immigrants looking to start their own businesses, there are several grant and loan programs available through government agencies such as the **Small Business Administration (SBA)**. These programs offer financial support to immigrants who want to open businesses, especially in underserved communities.
- **Tax Assistance**: Immigrants may be eligible for tax credits and deductions, depending on their status. The **Volunteer Income Tax Assistance (VITA)** program offers free tax preparation services to low-income immigrants, helping them file taxes and understand their tax responsibilities in the U.S.

Conclusion

The United States offers a variety of resources and support systems to assist immigrants in their journey to settle and integrate into their new homeland. By leveraging community organizations, legal aid, government services, and financial support, immigrants can successfully navigate the challenges of life in the U.S. and build a secure and prosperous future. Whether you need legal assistance, language classes, financial advice, or simply a sense of community, there are resources available to help you every step of the way.

End of Chapter 6.

Chapter 7: Navigating Challenges

Immigrating to a new country is a transformative experience, but it inevitably comes with a set of challenges that must be faced head-on. From navigating cultural adjustments to overcoming legal hurdles, these obstacles can seem daunting. However, with the right knowledge and strategies, you can not only address these issues but also thrive in your new environment. This chapter provides a detailed look at the most common challenges immigrants face in the United States and offers practical advice on how to navigate them successfully.

7.1 Cultural Adjustment

1. Understanding Cultural Differences

Cultural Norms and Etiquette:
Cultural norms in the U.S. can differ significantly from those in other countries, and understanding them is key to integrating into American society. For instance, the U.S. has a relatively informal and individualistic culture where people place a high value on personal freedom and equality. In social settings, people tend to address each other by their first names, even in professional or formal situations, which may feel unusual depending on where you're from.

Another important aspect of cultural adjustment is communication style. Americans often prefer direct communication, where people express themselves clearly and succinctly. In workplace settings, this translates to open feedback, including constructive criticism. While it may seem blunt, this style aims for efficiency and clarity.

Social Practices:
Certain everyday social practices in the U.S. may be unfamiliar. For example, tipping in restaurants and other service-oriented establishments is standard practice, usually 15-20% of

the total bill. Failing to tip may be considered rude, as service workers often depend on tips for a substantial part of their income.

Another custom to be mindful of is greeting etiquette. A handshake is the typical way of greeting someone in professional settings, while in casual situations, a simple "Hi" or "Hello" often suffices. Hugs or kisses on the cheek, common in some cultures, may not be as common unless you've developed a personal relationship with the individual.

2. Coping with Culture Shock

Recognizing Symptoms:
Culture shock is a psychological reaction to the unfamiliar customs, behaviors, and social norms of a new country. It often manifests as feelings of confusion, frustration, or homesickness. Initially, everything may seem exciting, but over time, you may start to feel isolated or disconnected. Recognizing these feelings as normal can help you manage them.

Symptoms of culture shock can include irritability, sleep disturbances, a sense of loss, or even a reluctance to engage with the new culture. Acknowledging these as part of the adjustment process will make it easier to work through them rather than letting them overwhelm you.

Strategies for Coping:
One of the most effective ways to cope with culture shock is to maintain connections to your cultural roots while gradually immersing yourself in American life. Engaging in activities such as cooking traditional meals, listening to familiar music, or speaking your native language can provide a sense of comfort.

At the same time, it's essential to remain open to new experiences. Embrace American traditions, explore local customs, and try to interact with people outside of your cultural community. The more you familiarize yourself with U.S. culture, the less disorienting it will feel over time.

3. Building a Support Network

Finding Community:
One of the most powerful tools for overcoming cultural adjustment challenges is building a strong support network. Seek out local immigrant communities or organizations that cater to newcomers. Many cities have cultural centers, churches, and community groups that host events for immigrants, offering opportunities to connect with people who share your background.

Social Activities:
Participating in local events, volunteering, or joining clubs and associations is an excellent way

to meet people and establish a sense of belonging. Many cities host cultural festivals, language exchanges, and other events where you can meet others with similar interests. By getting involved, you can expand your social circle, feel more connected to your new environment, and find others who may be going through similar experiences.

7.2 Bureaucratic and Legal Hurdles

1. Navigating Immigration Processes

Dealing with Paperwork:
Immigration to the U.S. involves extensive paperwork, and staying organized is critical. From visa applications to green card renewals, the process can be overwhelming. Keep copies of all your important documents, such as birth certificates, passports, and tax returns. Having a dedicated folder—both physical and digital—will make it easier to retrieve necessary documents when needed.

Seeking Help:
If you're unsure about the paperwork or processes, don't hesitate to seek help. Immigration attorneys or non-profit organizations that specialize in immigration services can guide you through the complexities of your specific situation. Legal aid organizations, such as the American Immigration Lawyers Association (AILA), provide resources and consultations for immigrants, often at reduced rates or even for free.

2. Addressing Visa and Status Issues

Overstays and Violations:
If you're in the U.S. on a visa, it's crucial to be aware of the expiration date and the conditions of your stay. Overstaying or violating the terms of your visa can lead to serious legal consequences, including deportation or being barred from re-entry. If you find yourself at risk of overstaying, consult an immigration attorney immediately to explore your options.

Status Adjustments:
In some cases, you may need to change or adjust your immigration status. For instance, if you entered the country on a student visa and now wish to work, you will need to apply for a status adjustment. The process typically involves submitting the appropriate forms to U.S. Citizenship and Immigration Services (USCIS) and providing the necessary supporting documentation.

3. Dealing with Bureaucratic Delays

Handling Delays:
It's common for immigration applications to face bureaucratic delays, which can be frustrating. Keep track of the status of your applications and check regularly for updates. USCIS has online tools that allow you to track the progress of your case. If you experience significant delays, you may want to follow up by contacting USCIS or even your local congressperson's office for assistance.

Documenting Communications:
Always keep a record of all communications with immigration authorities. This includes emails, letters, receipts, and even phone call logs. In case of any disputes or confusion, having a documented history can help resolve the issue more efficiently and prevent miscommunication.

7.3 Financial and Employment Challenges

1. Managing Finances

Budgeting and Expenses:
Financial management is one of the most critical aspects of settling in the U.S. One of the first steps is creating a budget that outlines your monthly income and expenses. Prioritize essential costs such as housing, utilities, groceries, transportation, and healthcare. Many immigrants find that the cost of living in the U.S. is higher than in their home countries, so adjusting your spending habits is essential.

Building Credit:
A good credit score is necessary for financial stability in the U.S., as it affects your ability to rent an apartment, buy a car, or even secure certain jobs. Start building credit by opening a bank account and applying for a secured credit card, which is easier to get for those with no credit history. Consistently paying your bills on time will help you establish and build your credit score.

2. Finding Employment

Job Search Strategies:
Finding a job in the U.S. can be challenging, especially if you're unfamiliar with the American job market. Use online job boards like Indeed or LinkedIn, as well as local employment agencies, to search for job openings. Networking is also crucial; attend job fairs, join professional organizations, and utilize platforms such as Meetup to connect with people in your industry.

Tailor your resume to meet U.S. standards by highlighting relevant experience and skills. Keep your resume clear and concise, and ensure that it reflects the qualifications and achievements that match the job you're applying for.

Overcoming Barriers:
Many immigrants face barriers to employment, such as unrecognized credentials or limited work experience in the U.S. In some cases, you may need to have your credentials evaluated by a specialized agency to confirm their equivalency to U.S. qualifications. Additionally, improving your language skills or obtaining additional certifications can enhance your employability.

3. Understanding Workplace Culture

Workplace Norms:
Workplace culture in the U.S. emphasizes punctuality, productivity, and collaboration. You are expected to be on time, meet deadlines, and communicate clearly with your colleagues. Teamwork and professionalism are highly valued, and it's important to maintain a respectful and cooperative attitude in the workplace.

Addressing Discrimination:
If you experience discrimination or unfair treatment at work, document all incidents in detail, including dates, times, and the people involved. You may choose to address the issue with your human resources department or seek advice from organizations such as the Equal Employment Opportunity Commission (EEOC), which enforces laws against workplace discrimination.

7.4 Health and Well-being

1. Accessing Healthcare Services

Health Insurance:
Health insurance is crucial in the U.S., as healthcare services can be expensive without it. If your employer doesn't offer insurance, explore options such as government programs (e.g., Medicaid, if you qualify) or private insurance plans available through the Health Insurance Marketplace.

Finding Providers:
Once you have health insurance, research providers who accept your insurance plan. It's advisable to establish a relationship with a primary care physician, who will oversee your general health care and make referrals to specialists as needed.

2. Managing Stress and Mental Health

Recognizing Stress:
The process of adapting to a new country can be mentally and emotionally taxing. Common symptoms of stress include irritability, fatigue, and difficulty concentrating. It's important to recognize these signs early and take action to manage them.

Seeking Support:
Don't hesitate to seek professional help if needed. Many cities have mental health clinics that provide free or low-cost counseling services. Community organizations and online resources also offer support for immigrants who may feel overwhelmed. Establishing a self-care routine—such as exercise, hobbies, or mindfulness activities—can also contribute to better mental well-being.

Conclusion

While the challenges of immigrating to the U.S. are real and varied, they are not insurmountable. By understanding cultural differences, navigating legal processes, managing finances, and prioritizing your well-being, you can overcome these obstacles and build a successful life in your new country. Remember that adaptation takes time, but with patience, persistence, and the right resources, you can thrive in your new environment.

End of Chapter 7.

Chapter 8: Pathways to Permanent Residency and Citizenship

Achieving permanent residency and U.S. citizenship is a crucial goal for many immigrants, marking the beginning of a stable and secure life in the United States. While the process may seem complex, understanding the pathways, requirements, and strategies involved can significantly ease your journey. This chapter will delve into the different avenues available to gain permanent residency (commonly known as a Green Card) and the steps to becoming a U.S. citizen through naturalization. We'll also discuss the potential challenges and offer practical advice to help you successfully navigate this important stage of your immigration process.

8.1 Pathways to Permanent Residency (Green Card)

Becoming a lawful permanent resident of the U.S. is an important step for immigrants, offering greater rights and stability, such as the ability to live and work permanently in the U.S. and providing a path to citizenship. Several routes lead to a Green Card, depending on your personal situation and background.

1. Employment-Based Green Cards

One of the most common ways immigrants obtain a Green Card is through employment. Employment-based Green Cards are divided into categories based on your occupation, qualifications, and skills.

- **Eligibility Categories**: Employment-based Green Cards are classified into preference categories:
    - **EB-1**: For priority workers, including individuals with extraordinary abilities in fields such as the sciences, arts, or business; outstanding professors and researchers; and certain multinational executives.
    - **EB-2**: For professionals with advanced degrees or exceptional abilities in certain fields. Applicants often require a job offer from a U.S. employer, though exceptions exist.
    - **EB-3**: For skilled workers, professionals, and unskilled workers. This category applies to those with specialized training or a bachelor's degree.
- **Application Process**: The application process begins with your employer filing a petition (Form I-140) with U.S. Citizenship and Immigration Services (USCIS) on your behalf. You may also need to go through the labor certification process to prove that no qualified U.S. workers are available for the position. After this, you can apply to adjust your status to that of a permanent resident (Form I-485) or undergo consular processing if you are outside the U.S.

The timeline and complexity of this process can vary depending on your job, employer, and country of origin. Consulting with an immigration attorney is often beneficial to navigate this detailed process.

2. Family-Sponsored Green Cards

Family-sponsored Green Cards are another primary pathway to permanent residency, allowing U.S. citizens and permanent residents to bring family members to the U.S.

- **Immediate Relatives**: U.S. citizens can sponsor their spouses, children under 21, and parents for Green Cards. Unlike other family-based categories, there are no annual limits for immediate relatives, making this process faster.
- **Other Family Members**: U.S. citizens can also sponsor siblings and adult children, while permanent residents can sponsor their spouses and unmarried children. However, these categories have annual limits, leading to longer wait times for visas.
- **Application Process**: For family-based Green Cards, the U.S. citizen or permanent resident sponsor must file Form I-130 (Petition for Alien Relative).

Once approved, the foreign relative can file Form I-485 to adjust their status if they are in the U.S., or undergo consular processing if they are abroad.

3. Diversity Visa Lottery

The Diversity Visa (DV) Lottery is a unique program aimed at individuals from countries with low immigration rates to the U.S.

- **Eligibility**: To qualify, you must be from an eligible country and meet minimum education or work experience requirements. Countries that have sent more than 50,000 immigrants to the U.S. in the last five years are excluded from the lottery.
- **Application Process**: You can apply online during the annual registration period. If selected, you will go through the visa application process, including submitting documents, attending an interview, and completing background checks. The DV Lottery is a highly competitive process, as millions of people apply for only 50,000 visas.

4. Asylum and Refugee Status

Immigrants who are granted asylum or refugee status can apply for a Green Card after living in the U.S. for one year.

- **Eligibility**: Asylum or refugee status is granted to individuals who have fled persecution or fear persecution in their home country based on race, religion, nationality, political opinion, or membership in a particular social group.
- **Application Process**: After holding asylum or refugee status for at least one year, you can file Form I-485 to adjust your status to a lawful permanent resident. You must meet continuous residency requirements and provide proof of your adherence to U.S. laws.

5. Investor Visas (EB-5)

The EB-5 Immigrant Investor Program offers Green Cards to individuals who make a substantial investment in a new commercial enterprise in the U.S.

- **Eligibility**: Investors must make a minimum investment of $1 million, or $500,000 in a targeted employment area, such as a rural area or a location with high unemployment. The investment must create at least 10 full-time jobs for U.S. workers.
- **Investment Requirements**: To qualify, the investment must be at risk, meaning there is a chance of loss, and it must result in job creation. EB-5 investors and their immediate family members can obtain Green Cards if the investment meets the program's criteria.

8.2 Applying for U.S. Citizenship

For many permanent residents, the ultimate goal is U.S. citizenship. Naturalization is the process by which immigrants become U.S. citizens. The process involves meeting certain eligibility criteria, completing an application, and passing a citizenship test.

1. Naturalization Requirements

Before applying for naturalization, it's important to understand the key requirements that you must meet:

- **Residency and Physical Presence**: To be eligible for naturalization, you must have been a permanent resident for at least five years (or three years if married to a U.S. citizen). You must also meet physical presence requirements, meaning you have lived in the U.S. for at least half of the required residency period.
- **Good Moral Character**: You must demonstrate good moral character, which generally means adhering to U.S. laws, paying taxes, and avoiding serious criminal offenses. USCIS reviews your history over the past five years (or three years for those applying based on marriage to a U.S. citizen).

2. The Naturalization Process

The naturalization process involves several key steps that require careful attention to detail:

- **Application (Form N-400)**: The first step is to file Form N-400 (Application for Naturalization) with USCIS. This form requires information about your residency, employment, and travel history. You will also need to submit certain documents and fees with your application.
- **Biometrics Appointment**: After filing your application, you will receive an appointment for biometrics. USCIS will collect your fingerprints, photograph, and signature to conduct background checks.
- **Interview and Test**: You will be required to attend an interview with a USCIS officer, during which you will be asked questions about your application and background. You will also take a civics and English language test, covering topics such as U.S. history and government.
- **Oath of Allegiance**: If your application is approved, the final step is to attend a naturalization ceremony, where you will take the Oath of Allegiance and officially become a U.S. citizen.

3. Special Circumstances

Certain individuals may qualify for expedited or special naturalization processes under specific conditions:

- **Military Service**: U.S. military members can be eligible for expedited naturalization if they have served honorably during periods of conflict. Military

service members should consult with their legal assistance offices for specific guidance on the application process.
- **Exceptional Cases**: Some individuals may qualify for citizenship through their parents or may be eligible for waivers of certain requirements due to medical conditions. Consult USCIS or legal counsel for further information on these special provisions.

8.3 Common Challenges and Solutions

The path to permanent residency and citizenship is not without its challenges, but understanding the potential roadblocks can help you prepare and overcome them.

1. Addressing Delays and Issues

Immigration processes are often lengthy, and you may face unexpected delays or requests for additional information.

- **Processing Delays**: It's not uncommon for immigration applications to take months or even years to process. Regularly check the status of your application through the USCIS website and follow up with USCIS if necessary.
- **Addressing Requests for Evidence (RFEs)**: If USCIS requests additional information or documentation (RFE), respond promptly and thoroughly to avoid further delays or denials. Make sure to provide the required evidence and any supporting documents.

2. Legal Assistance

If you encounter complex issues during the application process, seeking legal help can make a significant difference.

- **Seeking Legal Help**: Consulting an immigration attorney can help clarify difficult legal questions and provide guidance on complex situations, such as visa overstays, status adjustments, or criminal records. An attorney can also represent you during legal proceedings.
- **Finding Resources**: Non-profit organizations, community centers, and legal aid groups offer free or low-cost legal services to immigrants. These organizations can provide assistance with everything from filling out forms to navigating immigration court cases.

3. Staying Informed

Immigration laws and policies can change, and staying informed is key to ensuring your application progresses smoothly.

- **Keeping Updated**: Follow USCIS updates, stay connected with immigrant advocacy groups, and consult with professionals as needed to stay informed of any changes in immigration law or procedures that may impact your case.

8.4 Long-Term Planning and Considerations

Beyond the immediate steps to secure a Green Card or citizenship, it's important to consider long-term planning for your life in the U.S.

1. Maintaining Your Status

As a permanent resident or citizen, you must maintain your status and comply with U.S. laws.

- **Green Card Holders**: You must continue to meet residency requirements to maintain your permanent resident status. Spending significant time outside the U.S. could result in abandonment of your residency.
- **Citizenship Rights and Responsibilities**: U.S. citizens enjoy several rights, such as voting in elections and serving on a jury, but they also have responsibilities like paying taxes and complying with laws.

2. Planning for Family

Once you obtain permanent residency or citizenship, you can sponsor family members for immigration. Plan ahead to determine when and how to bring your loved ones to the U.S. through family-sponsored Green Cards.

- **Sponsoring Family Members**: As a U.S. citizen, you can sponsor a wider range of family members than as a permanent resident, so consider the timing of your naturalization.

3. Financial and Career Considerations

Achieving permanent residency or citizenship can open new financial and career opportunities. Permanent residents and citizens often qualify for additional benefits, such as access to financial aid for education or employment in government positions.

- **Building Credit**: Establishing and maintaining good credit in the U.S. is critical for future financial stability, such as when applying for loans or buying a home.
- **Advancing Your Career**: Citizenship may open doors to more career opportunities, such as jobs requiring security clearances or positions with federal agencies.

Conclusion

Gaining permanent residency and citizenship in the United States is a rewarding but often complex process. Whether you're pursuing a Green Card through employment, family sponsorship, asylum, or another route, it's important to understand the requirements and steps involved. Naturalization, too, comes with its own set of challenges and benefits. By staying informed, seeking legal advice when necessary, and planning ahead, you can successfully navigate this crucial stage in your immigration journey.

End of Chapter 8.

Chapter 9: Resources and Support

Successfully immigrating to the United States is an intricate and often challenging process. From navigating legal paperwork to integrating into a new society, immigrants can benefit from a wide range of support services and resources. These include government agencies, non-profit organizations, community-based initiatives, and online tools, all designed to assist you in your journey. This chapter explores these resources in detail, helping you understand what's available and how to access the support you need for a successful transition.

9.1 Government Resources

Government agencies are key players in managing and regulating the immigration process. Knowing which agencies provide relevant services can make a significant difference in navigating the system effectively.

1. U.S. Citizenship and Immigration Services (USCIS)

USCIS is the primary agency responsible for overseeing lawful immigration to the U.S. They offer a wealth of resources to help you navigate everything from visa applications to citizenship.

- **Website and Online Tools**: The USCIS website (uscis.gov) is a comprehensive resource. It offers detailed information on immigration processes, forms, and policies. You can use their online tools to:
    - **Check Application Status**: This allows you to monitor your application's progress through the system, ensuring you stay informed and can address any issues that arise.
    - **Form Instructions**: The website provides downloadable forms with clear instructions, ensuring you submit all required documentation correctly.

- ○ **Self-Service Tools**: USCIS's interactive tools help answer common questions about eligibility, case processing times, and more.
- **Local Offices**: USCIS has local field offices throughout the country where you can schedule appointments for in-person services such as interviews, biometrics collection, and consultations. These services are integral to completing the immigration process and are especially important if your case requires direct interaction with USCIS officials.

2. Immigration and Customs Enforcement (ICE)

ICE is responsible for enforcing immigration laws, specifically through its Enforcement and Removal Operations (ERO) division.

- **Enforcement and Removal Operations (ERO)**: ERO manages immigration enforcement, including deportation proceedings. If you or a loved one is involved in deportation proceedings, ERO provides information on your case status, legal rights, and the steps you can take. Although ICE is often associated with enforcement, understanding their procedures can be crucial if you're facing legal challenges related to immigration status.

3. Department of State

The U.S. Department of State oversees embassies and consulates abroad, handling immigration matters that occur outside of the U.S.

- **Consular Services**: If you are applying for a visa from outside the U.S., you'll likely work with a U.S. embassy or consulate. These offices handle visa interviews, consular processing, and offer general guidance for international immigration cases. If you need to renew a visa or attend an interview, the Department of State's resources are invaluable for tracking appointments and application statuses.

4. Legal Aid Resources

For immigrants seeking legal protection, especially refugees and asylum seekers, legal aid is a lifeline.

- **Office of Refugee Resettlement (ORR)**: ORR offers crucial services for refugees, asylees, and other vulnerable populations. They provide resettlement assistance, including help finding housing, jobs, and healthcare. Access to these services is crucial for starting a new life in the U.S., especially for those fleeing persecution or disaster.

9.2 Non-Profit Organizations

Non-profit organizations are often at the forefront of providing direct support to immigrants. These groups advocate for immigrant rights, provide legal assistance, and offer services ranging from language classes to job training.

1. Legal Aid Societies

Many non-profits and legal aid organizations offer free or low-cost legal services to immigrants who need help navigating the complex legal landscape.

- **Immigration Law Clinics**: These clinics, often associated with non-profits or universities, offer free or low-cost legal representation. They can help you with various issues such as visa applications, deportation defense, or family petitions. Organizations like the **Legal Aid Society** and the **Immigration Advocates Network** offer directories and connections to legal help across the country.

2. Advocacy Groups

Advocacy groups work to protect immigrant rights through legal challenges, policy reform, and public awareness campaigns.

- **American Civil Liberties Union (ACLU)**: The ACLU is deeply involved in advocating for immigrant rights, particularly regarding detention conditions, deportation cases, and discrimination. They offer resources to understand your legal rights and provide pathways to challenge unlawful actions.
- **National Immigration Law Center (NILC)**: NILC focuses on defending and advancing the rights of low-income immigrants. They play a pivotal role in legal advocacy and policy reform, particularly regarding access to health care, employment rights, and education for immigrants. Their resources can be helpful for understanding legal protections available to you, especially if you're navigating employment issues or seeking public benefits.

3. Community Organizations

Local community organizations provide an on-the-ground network of support for immigrants, offering services tailored to their specific needs.

- **Local Immigrant Support Centers**: These centers, found in most major cities, offer language classes, job placement services, cultural orientation programs, and other support to help immigrants settle into their new communities. These organizations are often staffed by people familiar with the challenges immigrants face and can provide personalized guidance.

4. Cultural and Ethnic Associations

Many cultural and ethnic associations are dedicated to helping immigrants from specific regions adjust to life in the U.S.

- **Ethnic Community Groups**: Whether you're from Mexico, India, China, or another country, you can often find community organizations that cater to immigrants from your home country. These groups offer social support, help maintain cultural traditions, and provide practical assistance such as finding housing, schools, or employment opportunities within the community.

9.3 Online Resources and Tools

The internet is a treasure trove of resources for immigrants, offering everything from practical advice on the application process to language-learning tools.

1. Immigration Information Websites

The internet provides a wealth of free information on immigration processes, often from the perspective of people who have already gone through it.

- **Immigration Forums and Blogs**: Online forums like Reddit's immigration threads or specialized immigration blogs can offer personal stories and practical tips. While not official sources, these platforms allow you to connect with others who have faced similar challenges, offering unique insights and solutions.
- **Government Websites**: Beyond USCIS, sites like the Department of State, Department of Labor, and Social Security Administration all offer crucial information for immigrants, including visa information, work permits, and social services.

2. Online Calculators and Checklists

Various websites provide interactive tools to help you determine your eligibility for different immigration benefits.

- **Eligibility Tools**: These online calculators assess whether you qualify for immigration benefits, such as green cards, visas, or citizenship. By inputting your personal data, you can quickly identify what pathways are available to you.
- **Application Checklists**: Many websites provide step-by-step checklists for different immigration processes, ensuring you gather all necessary documents and meet all deadlines.

3. Language and Integration Tools

Mastering English is one of the most important steps to integrating into American society, and many resources exist to help you improve your language skills.

- **Language Learning Apps**: Apps like **Duolingo**, **Babbel**, and **Rosetta Stone** are convenient tools for learning English. They offer lessons in grammar, vocabulary, and pronunciation to help you get conversationally fluent.

- **Integration Resources**: Beyond language, integration into American society involves understanding cultural norms, social practices, and even basic living tips. Online resources provide guides to everything from opening a bank account to understanding the U.S. healthcare system.

9.4 Educational and Professional Development

Education and career development are critical for long-term success in the U.S. Many immigrants find that expanding their skills or pursuing further education opens doors to better job opportunities and personal growth.

1. Continuing Education

Many immigrants pursue education in the U.S., whether to learn English, gain vocational training, or complete a degree.

- **Community Colleges and Universities**: Many community colleges and universities offer programs specifically designed for immigrants. These programs can include English as a Second Language (ESL) courses, vocational training, and even pathways to higher education degrees. Community colleges are particularly affordable and accessible options for immigrants seeking to further their education.
- **Online Courses**: Platforms like **Coursera** and **edX** provide a wealth of online learning opportunities. You can take courses from prestigious universities on subjects ranging from business to technology, often for free or at a low cost. These online platforms also offer certifications that can boost your resume and improve your job prospects.

2. Job Search and Career Services

Finding a job is often a top priority for immigrants. Fortunately, numerous organizations offer assistance with job searches, resume writing, and career development.

- **Employment Agencies**: Many employment agencies specialize in assisting immigrants with job placement. They help immigrants prepare resumes, practice for interviews, and match them with jobs suited to their skills. Some agencies also offer training programs to help immigrants qualify for higher-paying jobs.
- **Professional Networking**: Joining professional organizations and networking groups is a great way to connect with others in your field. Networking is an essential part of career advancement in the U.S., and building connections can lead to job opportunities or mentorships. Groups like LinkedIn or industry-specific associations are valuable tools for building your professional network.

3. Business Resources

For those with entrepreneurial ambitions, the U.S. offers numerous resources to help immigrants start and grow their own businesses.

- **Entrepreneurial Support**: Immigrant entrepreneurs can access support from small business development centers, which offer mentorship programs, business plan assistance, and funding opportunities. Government-backed programs like **SCORE** provide free mentoring and workshops on how to start a business in the U.S.

9.5 Health and Social Services

Understanding the U.S. healthcare system can be daunting, especially if you're coming from a country with a vastly different system. Fortunately, there are many resources designed to help immigrants access healthcare and social services.

1. Healthcare Access

Healthcare in the U.S. is often expensive and complex. However, immigrants are eligible for certain public health programs and services.

- **Health Insurance**: The Affordable Care Act (ACA) has expanded access to health insurance for many immigrants. Depending on your immigration status, you may qualify for Medicaid, the Children's Health Insurance Program (CHIP), or subsidies to help cover the cost of private insurance through the Health Insurance Marketplace.
- **Community Health Centers**: Community health centers across the U.S. provide medical care on a sliding fee scale based on income, regardless of immigration status. These centers offer essential services such as primary care, prenatal care, and dental services at an affordable cost.

2. Social Services

Immigrants can also access a range of social services to support their basic needs.

- **Food Assistance**: Immigrants may qualify for programs like **Supplemental Nutrition Assistance Program (SNAP)** or local food banks, depending on their legal status and income. These programs help ensure you and your family have access to nutritious food during times of need.
- **Housing Assistance**: Some immigrants are eligible for housing assistance programs that offer rental subsidies, public housing, or assistance with finding affordable housing options.

9.6 Cultural Adjustment Support

Adapting to a new culture is one of the most significant challenges immigrants face. Culture shock can lead to feelings of isolation or anxiety, but there are resources available to help you navigate the transition.

1. Counseling Services

Mental health support is crucial during the immigration process. Many organizations offer counseling services to help immigrants deal with the emotional and psychological challenges of adjusting to a new culture.

- **Cultural Adjustment Counseling**: Services like **Refugee Mental Health** or immigrant-focused counseling centers provide emotional support for those struggling with culture shock, trauma, or the stress of immigration. Mental health professionals can help you develop coping strategies and offer a safe space to discuss your experiences.

2. Cultural Orientation Programs

Cultural orientation programs are designed to introduce immigrants to American life, including its customs, values, and systems.

- **Community Integration Workshops**: Many local organizations offer workshops that cover topics like U.S. cultural norms, communication styles, and practical tips for living in American society. These programs help you feel more confident in navigating everyday situations, from grocery shopping to interacting with your neighbors.

Conclusion

In summary, numerous resources are available to support your immigration journey, from government services and legal aid to community support and educational tools. Leveraging these resources can help ease the transition and lay the groundwork for a successful and fulfilling life in the U.S.

End of Chapter 9.

Chapter 10: Real Stories and Case Studies

Understanding the complexities of immigrating to the United States can be daunting, but there is much to be learned from the experiences of others who have successfully navigated the process. Each immigrant's story is unique, marked by their challenges, strategies, and triumphs. In this chapter, we will explore real stories and case studies from diverse individuals, highlighting practical lessons and common obstacles. Their journeys offer not only inspiration but also valuable insights into the pathways available to aspiring U.S. residents and citizens.

10.1 Story 1: Maria's Journey from Refugee to Entrepreneur

Background:

Maria's story begins in a small village in Central America, where political instability and violence had become a daily reality. Fearing for her life and the safety of her family, Maria fled her home country and sought asylum in the United States. Upon arrival, she was granted refugee status, which marked the beginning of her journey toward permanent residency and eventually U.S. citizenship. However, the road ahead was fraught with difficulties.

Challenges Faced:

1. **Language Barrier:** English was not Maria's first language, and she struggled to communicate in her new environment. This language barrier made it difficult for her to navigate everyday life and understand the complex legal processes surrounding her refugee status. Filling out paperwork, communicating with government officials, and even engaging in simple tasks like grocery shopping were all made more challenging by her limited English proficiency.
2. **Employment:** Finding stable employment was another major obstacle. In her home country, Maria had been a skilled cook, but in the U.S., her lack of local work experience and professional networks made it difficult to secure a job. Her refugee status also posed challenges, as many employers were unsure about her work eligibility.

Path to Success:

1. **Community Support:** Determined to build a new life for herself and her family, Maria sought out local refugee support organizations. One organization, in particular, became a lifeline for her. They offered free English language classes, job training programs, and assistance with legal matters. Through their guidance, Maria gradually improved her English and began to understand how to navigate the immigration system.
2. **Entrepreneurship:** Maria's turning point came when she attended a small business development program offered by the same support organization. Drawing on her culinary background, Maria decided to start a catering business specializing in dishes from her home country. With the help of a microloan and mentorship, Maria launched her catering business, which quickly gained popularity in her community.

Outcome:

Through perseverance, Maria was able to adjust her refugee status to permanent residency. After several years, she became a naturalized U.S. citizen. Her catering business has grown significantly, and she now employs several other refugees. Maria is also an active community leader, volunteering her time to help other refugees who face similar challenges. Her story is a testament to the importance of community support and the power of entrepreneurship in transforming lives.

10.2 Story 2: Ahmed's Path to Citizenship Through Employment-Based Visa

Background:

Ahmed was an IT professional living in India when he received a job offer from a major U.S. tech company. This opportunity allowed him to apply for an H-1B visa, a temporary visa for skilled workers. Eager to advance his career and provide a better life for his family, Ahmed moved to the U.S. However, the process of transitioning from an H-1B visa to permanent residency and ultimately citizenship was not without its challenges.

Challenges Faced:
1. **Visa Cap Limits:** Ahmed's journey was complicated by the annual cap on H-1B visas, which limited the number of available visas each year. Additionally, green card quotas for applicants from countries like India were significantly backlogged, resulting in long wait times. For years, Ahmed had to live in uncertainty, unsure when or if his application would be approved.
2. **Family Separation:** During the initial stages of the application process, Ahmed's family remained in India. Being separated from his wife and children for extended periods was emotionally challenging. The slow pace of the visa and green card approval process only prolonged this difficult separation.

Path to Success:
1. **Legal Guidance:** Ahmed quickly realized that navigating the complex U.S. immigration system required professional legal assistance. He hired an experienced immigration attorney who specialized in employment-based visas. With his attorney's guidance, Ahmed was able to expedite parts of the application process and avoid common pitfalls that could have delayed his case.
2. **Networking:** Another key factor in Ahmed's success was the strong professional relationships he built within the tech industry. His employer advocated on his behalf, helping to secure the necessary paperwork and offering support throughout the green card application process. Ahmed's dedication to his work and his ability to network within his industry played a significant role in speeding up the green card process.

Outcome:

Ahmed eventually received his green card, and after five years of permanent residency, he applied for U.S. citizenship. He is now a U.S. citizen, a senior IT manager, and an active mentor to other immigrants in the tech field. Ahmed's story highlights the importance of legal guidance, professional networking, and perseverance in navigating the employment-based immigration process.

10.3 Story 3: Liu's Experience as a Family-Based Immigrant

Background:

Liu, a Chinese national, met her future husband, a U.S. citizen, while he was working abroad. After they married, Liu applied for a family-based green card to join her husband in the U.S. She arrived as a conditional permanent resident, meaning her residency was contingent upon the authenticity of her marriage and meeting specific legal requirements.

Challenges Faced:

1. **Cultural Adjustment:** Upon arriving in the U.S., Liu experienced significant cultural adjustment challenges. Everyday tasks that were once familiar became foreign, and she found it difficult to connect with others in her new community. The differences in cultural norms, language, and lifestyle made the transition more challenging than she had anticipated.
2. **Conditional Status:** As a conditional permanent resident, Liu's legal status was not guaranteed. She needed to prove the authenticity of her marriage, which required substantial documentation and legal work. The thought of potentially losing her residency if the conditions weren't met added significant stress to her life.

Path to Success:

1. **Support Groups:** Liu found solace in a local cultural exchange group that connected immigrants from different countries. The group offered support and advice for adjusting to life in the U.S., and it provided a space for Liu to share her experiences. Through the group, Liu made friends, practiced her English, and learned about American customs, which helped ease her transition.
2. **Documentation:** To remove the conditions on her green card, Liu and her husband meticulously documented their life together. They kept records of joint financial accounts, shared photos, and collected letters from friends and family attesting to the authenticity of their marriage. This thorough documentation made the removal of conditions process smoother.

Outcome:

Liu successfully removed the conditions on her green card, and after several years of permanent residency, she became a U.S. citizen. Today, Liu works as a community liaison, helping other immigrants adjust to life in the U.S. Her story underscores the importance of cultural support networks and diligent legal preparation when navigating the family-based immigration process.

10.4 Story 4: Omar's Asylum Journey

Background:

Omar, a native of Syria, fled his home country during the height of the Syrian civil war. Fearing persecution and violence, he sought asylum in the United States. His journey to permanent residency involved a lengthy and complicated asylum application process, followed by years of adjustment to life in a new country.

Challenges Faced:
1. **Legal Hurdles:** Omar's asylum application was filled with challenges. The process required extensive documentation to prove his fear of persecution, including evidence of his personal circumstances and the conditions in Syria. The backlog of asylum cases in the U.S. further delayed his case, leaving him in a state of legal limbo for years.
2. **Mental Health:** The trauma of fleeing his home, combined with the uncertainty of his legal status, took a toll on Omar's mental health. He struggled with anxiety, depression, and the emotional strain of being displaced from his family and country.

Path to Success:
1. **Professional Assistance:** Omar was fortunate to connect with a non-profit organization that specialized in asylum cases. They provided him with legal representation and helped him gather the necessary evidence to support his asylum claim. The organization also connected him with social services that offered emotional support during this challenging time.
2. **Community Involvement:** In addition to legal assistance, Omar became involved with local community services that helped him address his mental health. He joined a support group for refugees, where he found comfort in sharing his experiences with others who had faced similar hardships. This sense of community helped Omar cope with the trauma of his displacement.

Outcome:

Omar was eventually granted asylum, and after several years, he adjusted his status to permanent residency. He is now an advocate for refugees and asylum seekers, sharing his story to raise awareness and provide support to others in similar situations. Omar's journey highlights the importance of legal representation and mental health support for asylum seekers navigating the U.S. immigration system.

10.5 Story 5: Aisha's Diversity Visa Success

Background:

Aisha, a young woman from Nigeria, won the Diversity Visa (DV) Lottery, which provided her with the opportunity to apply for a green card and move to the United States. Excited to start a new life, Aisha was eager to take advantage of the opportunities the U.S. had to offer. However, the process of securing her green card through the DV Lottery posed several unexpected challenges.

Challenges Faced:

1. **Document Preparation:** Although winning the DV Lottery was a stroke of luck, the application process was far from simple. Aisha needed to gather a significant amount of documentation to prove her eligibility, including her birth certificate, education records, and police clearances. Collecting these documents in Nigeria proved to be time-consuming and difficult, especially with the bureaucratic hurdles in place.
2. **Interview Anxiety:** After submitting her documents, Aisha was scheduled for an interview at the U.S. embassy. The interview process was intimidating, as she needed to convince the consular officer that she met all the eligibility requirements for the DV Lottery. The fear of being denied a visa after winning the lottery weighed heavily on her.

Path to Success:

1. **Thorough Preparation:** To ensure a successful application, Aisha meticulously prepared for her interview. She double-checked her documents, practiced her responses to potential interview questions, and sought advice from others who had successfully gone through the DV Lottery process. Her attention to detail paid off during her interview.
2. **Persistence:** Aisha's persistence and determination helped her navigate the challenges of the DV Lottery process. Despite the initial difficulties in gathering documents and the anxiety surrounding her interview, she remained focused on her goal of immigrating to the U.S.

Outcome:

Aisha's visa was approved, and she successfully immigrated to the U.S., where she is now pursuing a degree in nursing. Her story demonstrates that even with the advantage of the DV Lottery, careful preparation and persistence are key to successfully navigating the U.S. immigration process.

10.6 Key Takeaways from Real Stories

1. **Seek Legal Guidance:** Whether through an attorney or a non-profit organization, having professional legal guidance is often critical to navigating the complexities of the U.S. immigration system.
2. **Community Support Matters:** Immigrants who seek out community support, whether through cultural groups, professional networks, or refugee organizations, often find it easier to adjust to life in the U.S. and overcome obstacles.
3. **Perseverance is Key:** The immigration process can be long and challenging, but perseverance often pays off. Those who stay focused on their goals, prepare thoroughly, and remain determined in the face of setbacks are more likely to succeed.
4. **Document Everything:** Whether applying for asylum, a family-based visa, or an employment-based green card, thorough documentation is critical. Keeping accurate records and providing detailed evidence can significantly strengthen an immigration case.
5. **Mental Health is Important:** The emotional strain of immigrating to a new country can be overwhelming. Seeking mental health support, whether through therapy or community groups, can make the adjustment process more manageable.

Conclusion

These real-life stories offer valuable lessons for anyone navigating the U.S. immigration process. From the importance of legal assistance to the power of community support, these case studies underscore the diverse challenges and opportunities faced by immigrants in the U.S.

End of Chapter 10.

Chapter 11: Conclusion - Your Step-by-Step Guide to Immigration Success

Congratulations! You've made it to the final chapter of *The Official Guide to Immigrating to the United States of America*. This book has walked you through every important aspect of the U.S. immigration process, and now it's time to summarize all of that knowledge into a clear, actionable step-by-step guide. This chapter will help crystallize everything you've learned, giving you a straightforward path to follow as you move forward in your immigration journey.

Step 1: Determine Your Immigration Path

Immigrating to the United States is not a one-size-fits-all process. The right path for one person may be completely different for another, and it's essential to begin by determining the immigration pathway that best fits your individual circumstances.

Assess Your Situation

Start by asking yourself *why* you want to immigrate to the U.S. Are you moving for employment opportunities, to reunite with family, or to seek asylum? Perhaps you've won the Diversity Visa Lottery, or maybe you're an investor looking to start a business. The reasons behind your decision will guide you to the appropriate immigration pathway.

There are several routes available, such as:

- **Family-Based Immigration**: For individuals who have immediate relatives in the U.S. who are citizens or lawful permanent residents.
- **Employment-Based Immigration**: For workers who have been offered jobs in the U.S. or have exceptional skills in their field.
- **Asylum**: For those who face persecution in their home country due to race, religion, political opinion, or membership in a particular social group.
- **Diversity Visa (DV) Lottery**: For individuals from countries with low rates of immigration to the U.S.

Review Eligibility Requirements

Each pathway comes with its own set of eligibility requirements. For example, family-based visas require proof of familial relationships, while employment-based visas often require a job offer from a U.S. employer. For asylum seekers, you must demonstrate a well-founded fear of persecution.

Before moving forward, take the time to carefully review the requirements for your chosen path. This step will help you avoid wasting time or money on an application for which you are not eligible. Look at the official U.S. Citizenship and Immigration Services (USCIS) website and other reliable sources to ensure you meet the qualifications.

Step 2: Gather and Prepare Documentation

Once you've determined the best path for your immigration, it's time to collect all of the documentation you'll need to support your application. Having the right documents is crucial to avoid delays and increase your chances of success.

Collect Essential Documents

Immigration to the U.S. involves meticulous record-keeping. Some of the common documents you may need include:

- **Passport**: A valid passport is mandatory for all immigration processes.
- **Birth Certificate**: Proof of your identity and nationality.
- **Marriage Certificate**: If applying as a spouse, this is critical to prove your marital status.
- **Financial Records**: You may need to demonstrate financial stability, especially for employment-based or investment visas. This could include bank statements, tax returns, or proof of employment.
- **Police Clearances**: For most visa categories, you will need to provide a police clearance certificate from every country where you've lived for six months or more after the age of 16.
- **Proof of Education or Work Experience**: If you are applying for an employment-based visa, you will need to show proof of your qualifications and experience.

Translate Documents

If any of your documents are not in English, you will need to have them translated by a certified translator. Make sure that both the original document and the translation are submitted as part of your application. Certified translations provide a statement from the translator verifying that the translation is accurate and complete.

Prepare for Interviews

Some immigration paths require in-person interviews at U.S. embassies or consulates. Preparation is key to success in these interviews. Be sure that your documents are well-organized and that you are familiar with the details of your case. Practice answering potential questions so that you can confidently explain your reasons for immigrating, your background, and your eligibility.

Step 3: Submit Your Application

With all of your documents prepared, you are ready to take the critical step of submitting your application. This process must be handled carefully to avoid errors that could cause delays or denials.

Complete Application Forms

Each immigration path has its own set of forms that must be filled out accurately and completely. Some examples include:

- **Form I-130**: For family-based petitions.

- **Form I-140**: For employment-based petitions.
- **Form DS-260**: For Diversity Visa Lottery winners.

Ensure that every question is answered, and double-check your forms for accuracy. Even small errors, such as incorrect dates or misspelled names, can cause your application to be delayed or rejected.

Pay Fees

Immigration applications often require the payment of various fees, including filing fees, biometrics fees, and visa fees. Be sure to follow the payment instructions carefully and keep copies of your receipts. Note that these fees are generally non-refundable, even if your application is denied.

Submit the Application

Once your forms are completed and your fees are paid, it's time to submit your application. Depending on the type of application, you may submit it online or via mail. Make sure you follow the specific submission instructions for your visa category and keep copies of everything you submit. It is always a good idea to use certified mail or another service that provides tracking and confirmation of receipt.

Step 4: Track Your Application

The waiting period after submitting your application can be stressful, but it's important to stay on top of the process by tracking your application and responding to any requests for additional information.

Check Status Online

USCIS and other immigration agencies provide online tools that allow you to check the status of your application. For USCIS applications, you can use the receipt number provided when you submitted your application to track your case online. Staying informed about the status of your application will help you anticipate any upcoming steps.

Respond to Requests

Sometimes, USCIS or the relevant agency will send a Request for Evidence (RFE) if they need additional information or documentation to process your application. Responding to these requests promptly and thoroughly is critical to avoid delays. Be sure to provide exactly what is requested, and double-check that your response is complete before submitting it.

Step 5: Attend Interviews and Biometrics Appointments

At certain stages in the immigration process, you may be required to attend interviews or biometrics appointments. These appointments are vital parts of the process and must be taken seriously.

Schedule and Prepare

You will receive a notice with the date, time, and location of any required interviews or biometrics appointments. Be sure to mark these dates on your calendar and plan ahead to avoid missing them. Missing an appointment can result in your application being delayed or even denied.

For interviews, review your entire application beforehand and bring all relevant documents with you. Be prepared to answer questions about your background, your reasons for immigrating, and your plans in the U.S.

Follow Instructions

At your appointment, follow all instructions provided by the USCIS officers or consular staff. Whether it's for biometrics (fingerprinting and photographing) or a formal interview, make sure you provide truthful, accurate information. Keep all correspondence from these appointments, as you may need them for future reference.

Step 6: Receive Decision and Take Action

After what may feel like a long wait, you will eventually receive a decision on your application. Whether the outcome is positive or negative, it's important to know how to proceed.

Review Decision

If your application is approved, you will receive your visa, green card, or other status documents. Carefully review these documents to ensure all the information is correct, including your name, visa category, and expiration dates.

Address Denials

If your application is denied, don't panic. Review the reasons for the denial carefully. In many cases, denials can be appealed or the application can be resubmitted with additional documentation. Depending on the reason for denial, you may need to seek legal advice to explore your options for reapplying or appealing the decision.

Step 7: Prepare for Relocation

Once your visa is approved, it's time to start planning your move to the U.S. This can be both an exciting and overwhelming step, so careful preparation is essential.

Plan Your Move

Start by making a checklist of all the logistics involved in your move. This includes securing housing, arranging transportation, and making financial preparations. If you're moving with family, you'll also need to arrange schools for children and any other necessary services.

Settle In

When you arrive in the U.S., take time to familiarize yourself with your new community. Find out what resources are available to immigrants, such as legal aid, healthcare services, and local cultural organizations. Taking advantage of these resources can help you adjust to your new environment more smoothly.

Step 8: Maintain Your Status

Your immigration journey doesn't end once you arrive in the U.S. It's crucial to maintain your legal status by understanding and fulfilling your responsibilities as a visa holder or permanent resident.

Understand Responsibilities

As a permanent resident or visa holder, you are required to follow certain rules to maintain your status. This may include:

- **Reporting changes in address**: You must notify USCIS of any change in your residential address.
- **Abiding by the terms of your visa**: If you're in the U.S. on a work or student visa, ensure that you continue to meet the conditions of your stay, such as remaining employed or enrolled in school.

Apply for Citizenship

If you're eligible for U.S. citizenship, you may consider applying once you meet the necessary residency and eligibility requirements. Becoming a U.S. citizen offers many benefits, including the right to vote and the ability to sponsor family members for immigration.

Your U.S. Immigration Journey Begins

With this guide, you now have a step-by-step roadmap to successfully navigate the U.S. immigration process. By staying informed, organized, and proactive, you can maximize your chances of success and begin a new chapter of your life in the United States. Best of luck as you embark on this exciting journey!

www.ingramcontent.com/pod-product-compliance
Lightning Source LLC
Chambersburg PA
CBHW070415230526
45471CB00006B/2813